Bushcraft And Survival Fire Lighting

Andrew Perrie

Andrew Perrie from Mad Dog Survival.

Copyright © 2021 by Andrew Perrie.

All rights reserved. This book or any portion thereof may not be reproduced or used in any manner whatsoever without the express written permission of the author except for the use of brief quotations in a book review.

Disclaimer: The information contained within this book is strictly for educational purposes. If you wish to apply techniques contained in this book you are taking full responsibility for your actions.

Some methods used in this book are only for reference and educational purposes only.

This book is dedicated to my YouTube friends.

My YouTube Channel is: Mad Dog Survival

Introduction

This book is designed to give the reader, who I'm assuming will already have a level of knowledge and experience in the bushcraft field, an extra "edge" when practising fire lighting in a bushcraft or survival situation, and is therefore not meant to be a full instructional manual for complete beginners, but more a reference guide to help with extra information such as tips/tricks some of which are not often explained elsewhere.

CONTENTS

[1] NEED FOR FIRE
[2] FUEL FOR THE FIRE
[3] FIRE LAY
[4] FEEDING THE FIRE
[5] METHODS
[6] FRICTION FIRE: THE BOW DRILL
[7] FRICTION FIRE: HAND DRILL
[8] FRICTION FIRE: THE FIRE ROLL
[9] SOLAR FIRE IGNITION
[10] FERROCERIUM RODS
[11] OPEN FLAME AND SPARKS
[12] FLINT AND STEEL
[13] CHEMICALS
[14] NEXT FIRE MENTALITY
[15] BUSHCRAFT
SURVIVAL HACKS AND TRICKS
[16] IN CLOSING

The Need For Fire

Fire forms one of the three sides of the survival triangle; without fire we cannot cook food, make water safe to drink, stay warm against the cold, signal for help, craft tools, and many other important needs. In a wilderness situation, fire can literally be the difference between life and death.
So with this in mind we outdoors people usually learn skills that allow us to be able to secure fire in several different ways.

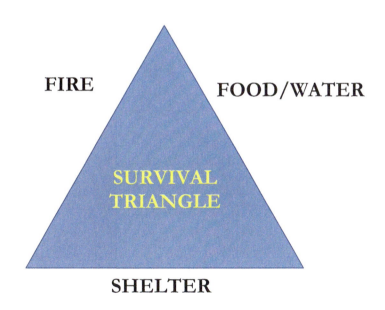

The Need For Fire

From modern instant flame devices
to primitive friction fires, we will look at these
methods in some detail and I will give hints, tips
and tricks to help improve your success
at fire lighting in the field.

Before moving on I truly believe
that a good base understanding of the fundamentals
of fire should be learned before we apply ourselves, so that
being said lets first look at the triangle of fire.

To maintain an effective and efficient fire
we must have three basic elements:

1: Air/Oxygen
2: Fuel
3: Ignition or Heat Source

The Need For Fire
Fire Triangle

Air contains Oxygen which is a gas required in sufficient quantities to allow for combustion to take place and be maintained

A source of heat or ignition which is sufficient to start the combustion process of a particular material

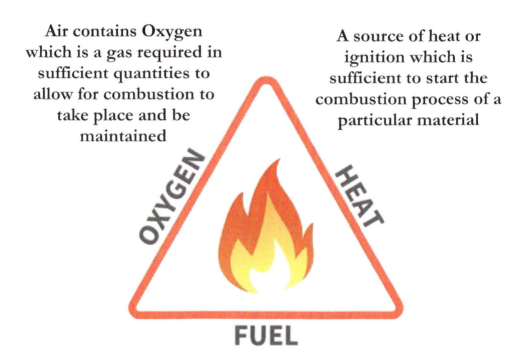

Material, which when heated sufficiently will reach flash point and combust, releasing energy in the form of heat and light

The Need For Fire

To explain a healthy fire lets think of a camp fire that is burning hot, bright, and with little or no smoke, this is a well balanced fire.

If we now add lots more wood of large sizes onto the flames we will see the flames slowly getting buried and suffocate and the fire begins to smoke heavily and start to die, at this point our fire is now in a fuel heavy oxygen light state, the triangle is broken. On the other hand if we now let the fire consume all the fuel until only ashes or embers are left, the fire also dies and this fire is in an oxygen heavy fuel light state, again the triangle is broken.

So knowing this, we need to find a perfect balance to maintain a hot and happy fire that emits little smoke.

Fuel For The Fire

Before we begin getting into the methods and techniques, it is also important to understand good practice of fuel selection, grading and types. The materials we choose should be graded into three categories.

These are:

1: Tinder
2: Kindling
3: Main fuel

Tinder is the first stage of igniting any fire, it should therefore be well prepared, dry and as fine as possible. This is going to take our initial ignition source, so it is important to be very selective and thorough when preparing any form of tinder.

For example, if are going to use an open flame method of ignition, e.g. a match, then using some fine strips of silver birch tree bark with added pine needles would be a good choice.

Fuel For The Fire

Kindling. This is the next stage of fuel and should be between pencil lead and pencil diameter sized pieces of dry wood and a good indication of perfectly dry wood is if it breaks cleanly with a crisp, sharp snap and does not bend or shred.

To find good kindling look for dead standing trees or plants/vines that are above knee height and are facing in a southern direction. Avoid picking off the ground as this will most probably contain lots of moisture, not good for our delicate young fire!

Main Fuel. As the name suggests, this will be our main fuel to maintain our fire; pieces from half an inch upwards in diameter, the intended use of our fire will be the deciding factor as to how large our main fuel will ultimately be.

Fire Lay

The base or lay of any fire is often an overlooked piece of the equation, as with many things in life attention to detail and proper preparation can make the difference between failure and success. The lay is basically dry pieces of fuel wood that are placed on the ground to raise the tinder and kindling up away from any potential moisture or snow.

The second purpose which is overlooked, is to ensure good airflow into the heart of the fire, and for this reason I recommend facing your lay into the direction of the prevailing wind. This will also ensure if you place yourself in front of your fire, any smoke will be carried away from you and not towards you!

Feeding The Fire

Once our lay is in place we should then make sure we have sufficient kindling and fuel to hand BEFORE lighting our tinder.

Tinder can be quick burning so it is important to be ready with extra fuel to hand once we begin. We do not want to be panicking, urgently looking around for anything in a hurried frenzied state, this can potentially be dangerous and at best will probably

end in our fire failing.
In my opinion, I like to have two good handfuls of kindling ready, one in each hand once our tinder is ignited. I will lay my kindling into the flames in a cross shaped fashion, allowing even-spacing to let plenty of air/oxygen to the base of the fire. I usually have at least the same amount on standby…
just in case.

Feeding The Fire

As a rule of thumb, once the flames have risen at least twice as high through the top of the initial kindling pile, it is then time to add more kindling or to start introducing larger pieces of fuel.
At this point, the fire should be well on its way and looking in good shape.

OK, we have covered the basic principles of good fire preparation now lets get to the good stuff!

Methods

There are several ways of causing heat to ignite a fuel source into combustion, these are as follows:

1: Friction
2: Solar
3: Chemical/Electrical
4: Open flame/Spark

In my opinion and experience, I would recommend to anybody who enjoys outdoor hobbies and pursuits in any form to carry at least three ways of starting a fire and there are many reasons for this as I will cover later on in this book.

Friction Fire

Can I take a minute here to give an opinion? Whilst primitive ways of fire lighting are a valuable skill to learn and master, and are an integral part of our bushcraft hobby it is at this point where I separate bushcraft from survival.

For me, bushcraft is the hobby of practising survival skills because I WANT to and inversely, survival is using bushcraft skills because I HAVE to. That being said, if you are ever unfortunate enough to find yourself in a true survival situation and calories in versus out will be the deciding factor of whether you live or die, you must always seek to use the most energy efficient way of fire lighting, so always carry a quality lighter and use this as your first option if possible.

However, this may not always be the case as we discuss later on.

Friction Fire
The Bow Drill

The Bow Drill is probably the most commonly used method of fire by friction. This set includes: The bow and cordage, a spindle or drill, a hearth board and catch pan, and a hand socket or bearing block.

Bow Drill set

Friction Fire

There are many opinions around this method and people get quite "passionate" when discussing correct technique, so I will not go into full tutorial on "how to" here. I will however give some useful Tips/Tricks that have worked for me over many years.

People often say that we should only make a bow drill set from the same type of wood, and whilst this works just fine, I prefer to make my kit from different woods if possible. The spindle/drill from a harder wood and the hearth board from softer wood.

As the name suggests bow DRILL, we are drilling into the hearth board to create a pile of fine dust that we ignite through a gradual increase in downward pressure and speed and therefore friction. This is how we achieve our ember.

The greater the dust pile, the larger the ember and hotter the coal will be that we transfer into our tinder bundle.

I usually look for pine for my hearth board and something like cherry or oak for my spindle or drill. Of course, this is my opinion and ultimately you must use what works best for yourself. There is no definitive right or wrong way.

Friction Fire

Nothing like a great camp fire!

Friction Fire

The bearing block or hand socket needs to be around palm size and it should be a comfortable fit but be large enough to apply downward pressure whilst still being easily controlled.

My recommendation would be to find a suitable piece of pine fat wood and carve a bearing block from this, ensuring the divot is smooth and not too deep.

Bearing block made from fat wood

Friction Fire

If you have carved your hand socket bearing block from wood, then use leaves, grass or mosses in the divot to act as a lubricant. Also Slugs and Snails make great emergency lubricants too!

You can also use cooking oils, greases, fats, lip balms, gun oils, Vaseline etc... any of these will help lubricate your bearing block.

Different types of bearing block

Friction Fire

This should ideally be approximately ten inches long and at least half an inch to one inch in diameter. I would recommend a used pencil like shape in profile as a rule of thumb.

Friction Fire
Tips/Tricks

1: Ensure that the friction end is almost flat with only a slight chamber to the edges to keep the spindle in the divot of the hearth board.

2: If your hand socket is getting hot or your set is squealing loudly, then this is a sign of your drill/spindle developing a shoulder at the bearing block end and will not spin freely. To remedy this, carve a steeper angle to a point like shape and try again. This is a common failure point I have seen many times.

3: Once you have initially "burned in" your set and are about to carve your "V" notch into the hearth board, take a moment to sand or carve away any glazing that may have formed at the friction end of the drill/spindle, do this prior to an actual fire run!

4: Never place your spindle/drill directly on the ground, especially the friction end, this will absorb moisture and make this even harder!

Friction Fire
Hearth Board or Fire Board

As stated, I personally prefer a softer wood for this as I feel it produces more of the dust we need to ignite by way of being drilled off by a harder spindle.

Here are my tips/tricks for your hearth board:

1: When carving your hearth board, use the centre portion of the log you split as this will be the driest!

2: The area where the divot is to be made should ideally be around half to three quarters of an inch deep. However this does not mean that the entire piece of wood needs to be carved this thin, if the board is left thicker away from the divot part, it will be easier to hold in place with your foot and means less work carving!

3: Foothold: Keep wet boots away from the friction divot area, and also be aware of your head position as sweat can easily drip onto the friction area too.

4: If you have charred material available e.g. char cloth, use some under your "V" notch on the catch pan and this will greatly extend your ember/coal!

V notch opened out for air flow under hearth board

5: Ensure the under side of the "V" notch has a chamber to allow good air flow to the dust pile that we are trying to ignite.

Bow and Cordage

The bow should be around finger tip to armpit in length, and be around half an inch to an inch in diameter, I prefer a bow with a slight bend, but a straight piece will work fine too.

Tip/Tricks: Use bank line over para cord as this will not stretch out as much or deteriorate as quickly

Friction Fire

Catch Pan

Your catch pan should be large enough for you to hold down whilst removing the hearth board after igniting our ember, obviously this piece has got to be absolutely dry!

Top tip! as before place a piece of charred material on the catch pan before drilling, this will act as a great coal extender.

Ember or Coal

Now we have our precious coal, now is the time to slow down, don't rush! gather your breath and wipe your brow. Always take your tinder to the ember, never the ember to the tinder!
Drop it now and its back to the start!

Friction Fire

Place your ember into your tinder bundle and hold it up and away from you, blow gently and slowly, give the ember time to transfer its heat into the tinder.

Once you have flame, turn the tinder bundle over as you move it onto your fire lay, this will let the flames rise through the tinder developing a good solid base! Time to relax, slowly load up your fire, then sit back and enjoy your work!

Turn the tinder upside down once flames are produced

Friction Fire
Hand Drill

The hand drill method is probably the most iconic image of survival fire lighting, yet in reality the bow drill is mechanically more efficient and effective. However the hand drill is a satisfying and rewarding skill to learn.

Here are tips/advice that have worked for me:

1: The spindle should be around 24-30 inches in length and I prefer a slight taper getting towards the friction end, this is because I feel it gives me a mechanical gearing advantage. If my hands are turning the upper thinner end of the spindle at a given rate then the lower wider friction end will be turning at the same rate but with a larger surface area and hence more friction.

2: Roll your hands in a scissor like motion to get the most stroke from each roll.

3: The hearth board needs to be thinner than that of the bow drill method as we do not have as much mechanical power to apply. Ideally around quarter of an inch works well.

Friction Fire

Hands rolling the spindle for efficient strokes

4: This information is something that is seldom spoke about on other survival platforms but the truth is, to be able to perform an effective hand drill friction fire, your set must be very well cured, which usually means being selected and then dry stored for over a year! This is why some tribes people often pass down hand drill pieces to their next generations. It is for this reason that I also prefer the bow drill, as with practice an effective set can usually be made and used on demand.

Friction Fire

5: Materials. Here are some good materials out of which make effective hand drill spindles:

1: Elder
2: Willow
3: Hazel
4: Oak
5: Yew
6: Sycamore

Hand drill fire set

My hazel spindle I have owned and used for many years

Friction Fire
The Fire Roll

Probably the easiest friction fire method to master, this method of fire lighting has an uncertain history as some people believe it to have originated from the second world war when troops used this to light their cigarettes.

However it is known to have been used before then by a survivalist named Rüdiger Nehber, hence one of its common name sakes the "Rudiger Roll". It is also known to have been used for hundreds of years in a similar fashion in the Philippines and is known there as the "Bohol Roll".

The basic principle of this method is to unroll a piece of cotton wool ball into a strip and onto this, add fine ashes from a previous fire. This is then re-rolled into a tight cigar like shape and rolled between two pieces of board to create friction ignition.

Friction Fire

Wood ash placed on cotton ball strip ready to re roll

The rolled up cotton "cigar" is now placed between the two boards and rolled with increasing pressure and speed until the ash acts as a catalyst for the cotton to reach its flash temperature and at this point you will have developed an ember and will smell it smouldering. You will now need to loosen the fibres to allow air to get to your ember and then place into your tinder bundle and blow to flame.

There are many other items that can be used for this method; rust, coffee, dry fungus, tobacco, dry herbs, and tea to name but a few!

Friction Fire

This method can also be performed using flat rocks or bricks as a board substitute. Split logs will work but they must be obviously dry.

Friction Fire

Once an ember is formed, let in air and place
into tinder bundle to blow to flame

There are several other methods of friction fire techniques such as the fire plough, bamboo plough, and pump drill method. The basic principles of these are essentially the same and I feel we need to move on to the next method.

Solar Ignition

The Sun, a fantastic resource that hopefully will not run out any time soon and because of this, we should take advantage of its free, non consumable using nature as often as we can. Using sun rays to cause the effect of fire is a great way of preserving our other resources that may be harder to come by.

Do we need a magnifying lens? Ideally yes, however there are many other options available for us to use if we have to. A good lens in my opinion should be 5X magnification and around 40 mm in diameter. Before we light our fire lets first look at other options of lenses.

Some examples of items that can be used to light fires by solar ignition

Solar Ignition

There are every day items we can use to effect solar ignition, some of these are include: Sandwich bag, condom, clear water bottle, dog bowl, a polished can bottom or even your compass.

Fresnel lenses work great too.

Tip: When using a Fresnel lens always remember the smooth side faces the sun and the layered rough side faces the material you intend to ignite!

Solar ignition works best with charred materials such as char cloth or charred punk wood, however we can also use other tinders too. We can use various fungus such as the horse hoof or Arthur's cake mushrooms to get a great coal developed, these are great ways of transporting fire from camp to camp too as they can smoulder away for hours in some cases.

Using a Solar lighter

Solar Ignition

Tip/Trick: Use a small amount of water in the bottom corner of a sandwich bag to create a lens, this can also be done with a condom.

A quick safety reminder. NEVER look directly into the Sun! Our eyes are precious and we only get one pair!

Blowing an ember from solar ignition into flame

Solar Ignition

Good Tinder Tips:
Anything that is made from 100 percent cotton material, dry animal dung (especially grazing stock as this will be mainly dried fibrous vegetation mass), climbing plants or vines, dry outer barks and rotten or punk wood pieces from dead standing trees.

Other Top Tips:
Charcoal from previous fires hold a great ember!

Also, did you know that burning some grazing animal dung on your camp fire will help keep the midges and mozzies away too!

Example of punk wood

The Ferrocerium Rod

The Ferrocerium Rod or Ferro Rod and also know as the fire steel, is a rod of pyrophoric alloy metals consisting of: Iron, Cerium, Praseodymium, Neodymium, Magnesium and Lanthanum.

When struck or scraped, these materials produce hot showers of sparks which burn at around 3000 degrees centigrade. Most manufacturers of ferro rod claim that these can be used/struck around 20000 times so making it a long life piece of kit.

This is my personal favourite and most valued fire lighting method as I feel its advantages are many over other methods, to include: it can be used in wet weather conditions and temperature does not affect its performance, it can be used with minimal calorific usage so not hard work in a survival situation, it is very durable and tough, and can last many years. I love the Ferro Rod so much I even produce my own on my eBay shop!

Open Flame and Sparks

In this section we are going to look at open flame equipment and spark generating tools and we will see the respective pros and cons along with some Tips/Tricks too.

The Common Lighter

The most obvious choice of equipment to carry to light a fire, however whilst I would always recommend carrying at least two good quality lighters, they also have their weak points and should not be totally relied upon. Have you ever got your lighter wet for example? Once the wheel is wet it will no longer light until it is thoroughly dried out, also as the butane boils in the air at temperatures above freezing to become a gas. So therefore, colder climates mean the flame produced (if at all) will be weak at best.

So if you are operating in a snowy environment, or are water borne like cannoning etc., a lighter should not be your only means of fire lighting, and if you need to dry yourself and your clothing out quickly to ward off the onset of hypothermia, a wet cold lighter is not an ideal situation to find yourself in especially with hands and fingers that probably are not as dexterous due to the cold!

Open Flame and Sparks

Elastic bands used to stop the accidental discharge of gas and empty lighters can still be used too!

Tips/Tricks

1: A good rule of thumb here is to hold the button down on your lighter for no longer than ten seconds, If a longer time is required it means your tinder is either improperly prepared or marginal (to mean wet or damp). The other issue with this is a temperature overload occurring which will result in the lighters valve potentially to fail, I would definitely recommend practising as it can be not as easy as one first thinks!

2: Empty lighters can still be used! Simply remove the silver wind shield to expose the wheel and flint workings of the lighter, now add a piece of cotton wool or field dressing to this area and strike it with sparks, instant fire! But again, prepare your tinder before igniting your cotton wool!

3: Use rubber bands to wrap around the button of your lighter this will prevent it accidentally being pressed and wasting the gas. The rubber bands are also an effective fire extender which are good in wet or humid environments.

Matches

Strike anywhere matches have been around since 1826 when John Walker of England produced the first safe production viable versions of a match. However matches have been used in the form of sulphur spills since at least the 1600's which were then developed to white phosphorus matches, these were unstable and dangerous to use as they had to be mixed with acid to cause combustion! hence why we now use a red stable form of phosphorus.

Examples of different match types

Open Flame and Sparks

With the more modern invention of the storm proof match, we have seen a whole variety of different types and styles on the market today, including the military "survival" matches through to enormous camp fire matches and whilst these definitely have their place and uses, I personally still prefer the standard old strike anywhere type of match, because I feel they burn with a slower and more controllable flame allowing for better placement into the tinder and more time too!

The obvious other reason is that standard matches come in boxes of 50+ and are much more cost friendly compared to the fancy storm proof matches usually numbering around 10-20 and several times the price.

A simple and effective way to improve any standard match is to dip the ends of the matches into molten wax or to paint the ends with nail varnish lacquer, this will waterproof your matches and make for better storage. I am personally not a big fan of matches to carry in my kit so I wont dwell here.

Open Flame and Sparks

Some examples of ferro rods and strikers

There are many styles of ferro rods and also prices too. My preferred size to use is the (5 inch X half inch) diameter as this is large enough to be easily handled whilst not being massive, that it weighs half a ton in your kit!

Moving onto Tips/Tricks: It is my opinion that the striker is just as important as the rod itself I would highly recommend a quality striker of either high speed steel or one of my Mad Dog Survival ceramic types as this also has other survival use

Open Flame and Sparks

In the unlikely but possible event of losing the striker for your rod, other items can be used as a substitute and some of these could be these:

The spine of your knife or back of a Swiss Army knife saw blade, a piece of flint or chert or any other mineral that is hard enough to scrape off ferro rod material, a shard of glass works well with caution, a piece of hacksaw blade, an oil stone or piece of old metal file. All of the above work fine in an emergency and is worth experimenting/practising with before the situation arises.

Examples of ferro rod strikers

Open Flame and Sparks

As always, good tinder preparation is key in using the ferro rod effectively and efficiently, the tinder needs to be as fine and opened fibred as can be. This is to create a larger surface area which will easily catch the hot sparks and will have sufficient air/oxygen to burn straight away.

Top Tip: Use a piece of duct tape or medical tape from your first aid kit folded over double to create a sticky base onto which you can place any fine tinders like magnesium shavings or fat wood curls without them being lost to the wind, this will also act as a fire extender too!

Use firm solid full length strokes of your ferro rod and don't lightly scrape it, remember we are trying to remove material that will continue to burn after the fact. Just making sparks that are already cooling before they hit your tinder is not what we need so do it like you mean it!

Open Flame and Sparks

If you are throwing sparks into fine tinder dust then try holding the striker over the tinder and pull the ferro rod backwards toward yourself, this will avoid knocking your tinder all over the place and risk losing it to the wind or it getting lost to the ground.

Ferro rod being used on fire lay

Some common and useful natural tinders we can use with a ferro rod are as follows:

Pine fat wood, silver birch bark, cedar bark fibres, dried fungus (such as the horse hoof mushroom), dry vine barks (make great tinder bundles), dry pine needles, tall dry grasses and cat tail seed pods from the water reeds.

Open Flame and Sparks

Another great technique we can employ is to make and use feather sticks, these are basically dry pieces of wood that we have carved down onto forming long curls that collect at the bottom of our wood.

They act as a tinder source that has the next stage of fuel already attached, they can be lit with a ferro rod, lighter or match. Because of the curls, these have a great surface area and lots of nice edges for our flames to get hold of easily.

In my opinion a valuable skill well worth learning and practising.

Feather sticks

Open Flame and Sparks

Tips/Tricks: Before moving onto Flint and Steel, here are some man made tinders and other items that can be used to effect fire from using a ferro rod.

1: Cotton balls with a little added Vaseline.
2: Car air freshener (card type) - scrape and ignite!
3: Make-up removal pads, dip into molten paraffin wax for a great waterproof fire lighting tinder.
4: Duraglit/Brasso polish, very flammable tinder.
5: Hand sanitiser (alcohol based), burns hot with a clear flame.
6: Wire wool can be lit with a ferro rod - add to tinder and your fire is done!
7: Brake open a sharpy type of marker pen, the ink filament is highly flammable!

Flint and Steel

Probably one of, if not the oldest known form of man-made intentional fire lighting methods.

There is evidence from the middle Palaeolithic times which spans 300,000 to 50,000 years ago that shows Neanderthals would have known about and used a basic form of this method. It is not certain exactly how or what materials they would have used but the most accepted theory is the use of pyrite rocks. Flint and Steel method is basically the technique of striking a piece of rock, usually flint or chert against a piece of high carbon steel in order to shave off tiny particles of the steel which through the friction causes it to burn in the air which we see as sparks. The rock therefore has to be hard enough to remove these tiny particles for this to work and a rule of thumb here is any mineral over the Mohs scale of 7 should work fine.

Some minerals which work well are as follows: Flints or Chert, Pyrites, Quartz (of which there are many) Amazonite, Tourmaline and Feldspar to mention but a few.

Flint and Steel

Example of a Flint and Steel kit

We need to remember that the sparks produced by this method are way cooler than that of the ferro rod. The ferro rods sparks burn at around 3000 degrees centigrade, where as the flint and steel sparks only around 800 degrees centigrade, so this means our tinder needs to be different in their flashpoint reactivity too.

Flint and Steel

As stated, this book is not designed to be a full tutorial, as I am assuming the reader has some experience with this subject, so again lets move on to some Tips/Tricks and advice for this method.

1: Once a spark has been caught onto our piece of charred material, don't rush this ember straight into your tinder bundle, first add some more charred material to your coal as this will extend the ember and transfer more heat for a longer time into your tinder. This is advantageous if your tinder is damp as it allows more ember burn time before being expended and lost before ignition is achieved.

2: Practice light glancing blows of your striker onto the flint until you can perform this without needing to look at the flint, this will quickly develop your skill set here!

3: You can use the spine of a carbon steel knife to throw sparks into your charred material, again another good reason to have a ninety degree spine on your knife.

Spine of knife being used to throw sparks into charred material

4: A good quality old steel file makes a great steel striker.

A piece of old metal file used as a striker

Flint and Steel
Top Tips

Poly-pore bracket mushrooms when dry make great tinder, as do the Arthurs cake fire fungus fungi.

To use these directly with no time consuming process, the easiest way is to take your saw and make cuts down into the mushrooms, being careful to keep the dust that is formed. This dust pile will then take a spark from flint and steel and form a nice useable ember.

The tinder Amadou is made from the inner layers of these mushrooms and is also one of the best tinders for flint and steel.

Bracket fungus for fire tinder

Chemicals

Before starting here I want to stress that this information is for reference and educational purposes only and only ever to be used in a true survival situation!

There are several ways of causing combustion using chemicals, we will look at a couple of the more common ways here and add a couple of extra Tips.

Most of us know that Potassium Permanganate is a great multi-use chemical that when mixed with the food additive glycerine, it will cause a violent reaction that results in combustion. Here are some extra tips for this method.

Potassium Permanganate being used to react into fire

Chemicals

Because Glycerine is the key component that reacts with potassium permanganate, we can also use other items that have a content of glycols within them, a few common ones are:

1: Automotive anti-freeze.
2: Automotive brake fluid.
3: Some medicines for sore throats also have a high content of glycerine and will work.

Examples that also react with potassium permanganate

Chemicals

As well as its fire making properties, lets not forget this chemical is also a great antibiotic, and antibacterial, so makes an ideal solution for treating athletes foot, or mouth ulcers, and can be used to purify water in an emergency.

The chemical reaction of potassium permanganate into combustion

The ambient temperature is also a key point using this method and an ideal temperature would be around 18 degrees centigrade, in colder temperatures the reaction is slower and in some cases will not combust, so this is worth remembering if you are ever in a situation were you need to rely on this!

Chemicals

Top Tip: Using a mortar and pestle, grind the potassium permanganate up finely before it is needed for use and this will make the reaction more effective. Another way of using this chemical to produce fire is to grind into it equal amounts of granulated white sugar, and with downward force this will result in a violent ignition. I do not recommend or endorse this.

Rub Cloth

Rub cloth was used by pioneers and troops of the 17th and 18th centuries, it is made by tacking a piece of cotton material (something like gun barrel cleaning swab) wetting this material piece and then rubbing into it black powder (gun powder) until the piece is entirely covered. This is then left to dry, and can then be ignited with any form of spark generated, the resulting flash of black powder burning, produces a hot glowing ember that after the initial flame is basically an instant way of producing charred cloth material, again this information is for reference only.

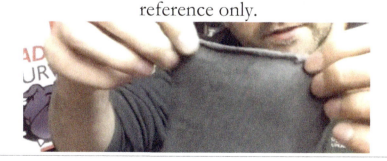

Chemicals

Rub cloths violent burn once ignited

The next methods are using batteries, I have included these in the chemical section as there are methods of fire lighting using the chemicals within a battery which I will cover later.

The first and most easily done way of fire lighting using a battery is to take some fine wire wool, put this into your tinder bundle, and then simply push the terminals of a 9 volt battery into the wire wool and this will cause an over current short-circuit which will ignite the wire wool and then your tinder.

See illustrations next.

Chemicals

Wire wool and battery fire setup

Igniting the wire wool with a battery

A similar method can be used using a AA or AAA type battery using a strip of gum wrapping foil paper as the material to cause the short-circuit and fire.

Chemicals

A portion of the foil paper gum wrapper needs to have a reduced area cut into it this will be the weak point that gets electrically overloaded and burns

The two ends of the foiled paper then need to be held across the battery terminals causing the short-circuit overload

Chemicals

The next chemical fire method involves using the actual content of a battery. For this method, an automotive car/truck battery is required and we need to be able to accesses the acid inside. For safety reasons I have demonstrated this using acid from a bottle on my work bench. This method is highly dangerous and is only here for reference! Automotive batteries use sulphuric acid which if mixed with a cellulose and an oxidising agent will react into a violent combustion. The procedure here is to use a piece of material which is made of glass, metal or man made synthetics to remove some drops of battery acid from the cells, these drops are then added to our friend potassium permanganate. DO NOT USE WOOD OR ANYTHING NATURAL as these will contain celluloses which is what will react.

We now add these drops of potassium permanganate acid infused drops onto a cellulose compound such as cotton wool, wood shavings or first aid dressings. This needs to be done quickly and with great care as the ensuing reaction is violent and fast! I demonstrated this method on my YouTube channel for educational purposes and I repeat this is for reference only. Illustrations next.

Chemicals

The violent reaction caused by battery acid on cellulose in conjunction with potassium permanganate

The resulting fire from the reaction

Chemicals

We can also include pyrotechnic devices such as flares, smoke grenades and ammunition in this section as they are items that we may have as part of a signalling kit or items we may have if hunting for example. All of these items can be used to light fire. An activated flare can obviously be held directly into a fire lay to ignite the tinder. Smoke devices and ammunition can be dismantled for their contents, using an open flame or spark device if necessary too.

A marine flare being used to light fire

Next Fire Mentality

Next fire mentality is in my opinion something that is often overlooked in our Bushcraft/Survival subject. When we go out into the wilderness with our chosen fire lighting tools we often forget that our planned outing could potentially end up being a longer duration than we had anticipated.

For example, if we were to get lost or have an injury then our supplies now need to last a lot longer until we either get help or find our way out. So for example if we are relying on our trusty lighter what happens once the gas has ran out? or if are using man made fire starting aids like my Mad Dog biscuits what do we do once they are all used up?

This is why I highly recommend using the next fire mentality which is about utilising the current fire to produce items that will help start the next fire. For this, you will need a tin with a good fitting lid. This will allow us to produce charred material such as cotton, punk wood or fungus etc.

Next Fire Mentality

The tin in conjunction with our flint and steel kit or solar ignition kit (magnifying lens) and we now have a way to create and re-create as many fires as we need with an unlimited amount of resource.
This is why my own fire kit that I choose to carry consists of these items as my main base layer:

1: Ferro rod and striker.
2: Flint and steel kit (does not have to be large).
3: Good quality lighter.
4: Magnifying lens.

The flint and steel kit and lens can be stored in the charring tin for easy storage.

Small, medium and large tins for charring materials showing flint and steel kit contents

Bushcraft Tips/Tricks/Hacks

In this last section I wanted to add a few Tips/Tricks/Hacks that are useful or fun, related to fire lighting. I hope you find them useful and interesting!

1: A simple stick of lip balm can act as a make shift candle or fire extender fuel in an emergency situation, rub some balm directly onto your kindling or a simple string wick to use as a candle

Lip balm emergency candle

Bushcraft Tips/Tricks/Hacks

2: Polystyrene and Acetone fuel. Polystyrene can be melted directly into Acetone to form a sticky fuel gel, this mixture is actually the base of what was used in early napalm! It can be used as a stove fuel or as a fire extender in wet conditions. Nail varnish remover has a high Acetone content and works well for this. Again, this is for reference only.

Acetone and Polystyrene used as fuel gel

Bushcraft Tips/Tricks/Hacks

3: Hand sanitiser can be used as stove fuel or a fire accelerant due to its high alcohol content and here it can be seen being used as a fuel for a rope stove.

Hand sanitiser being used as stove fuel

4: Boot polish can be used as a great fire lighter, take a small piece out of the tin and place onto your tinder, light with either open flame or spark and this will act as a fire extender.

Bushcraft Tips/Tricks/Hacks

5: Bird feathers can sometimes be found after an animal or bird of prey has taken a bird for food, these feathers especially downy feathers can make a good flash tinder when dry, smelly but effective!

6: First aid alcohol wipes or swabs can be used for an easy ignition source again due to the high alcohol content. These can be lit with spark or open flame. Most field dressings make great tinder too, but any first aid item must only be used as a last resort. You may need it!

7: As we know from earlier in this book, potassium permanganate reacts violently into combustion when mixed with anything that is glycol based so here is another one that works well. E-cigarette fluid is mainly glycerine and works well with this method.

Bushcraft Tips/Tricks/Hacks

8: Clothing. Some modern clothing items are filled with synthetic padding or insulation materials that are highly flammable and whilst we normally take care not to get too close to a fire when wearing these items, we can also use this to our advantage in an emergency situation. Take a small amount of the inner material from your clothing item and use as a tinder, this can then be lit with spark or open flame.

Inner fleece jacket material being used as emergency tinder

Bushcraft Tips/Tricks/Hacks

9: Hexamine fuel blocks can be lit using a ferro rod if you have no matches or lighter. Use your striker or knife to scrape the surface of the fuel block into a fine powder, this can then be lit by throwing sparks into this dust pile from your ferro rod.

Hexi block being scraped for ferro rod ignition

Bushcraft Tips/Tricks/Hacks

10: Buddy burner improvement. Most of us outdoors people will be familiar with the buddy burner, this is a basic stove made from a can/tin bottom filled with layers of rolled up cardboard which are then covered with molten wax to form a fuel cell. My little Tip here is to use a piece of cotton ball in the centre of your burner and with this way you can now light it with both ferro rod and open flame methods.

Buddy burner using cotton centre for easier ignition

In Closing

In closing this little book I would like to thank you all for your kind support both here and on my YouTube channel.

I have tried to make this my first attempt at publishing light reading without drawing the subject out into too much detail. If anyone has any questions or would like more information please drop me a message on my channel comments box and I will do my best to help in anyway I can.

Again, thank you very much. I hope you have picked up a few Tips or Tricks that may help you in your fire lighting adventures for our Bushcraft hobby.

Best wishes all.

Printed by Amazon Italia Logistica S.r.l.
Torrazza Piemonte (TO), Italy